Breaths of Life

Invite Yourself to Live Again

And the Lord God formed man...and breathed into his nostrils the breath of life; and man became a living soul.
Genesis 2:7

All scripture quotations are taken from the King James Version of the Holy Bible

Photos by Erika Morgan & Ci'Airah Thomas

Copyright © 2014 Erika Morgan
All rights reserved.
Contents may not be reproduced in whole or in part in any form without the express written consent of the author.
ISBN: 0692212205
ISBN-13: 9780692212202

Dedication

This book is dedicated to God for ALWAYS breathing life into me during the times when I couldn't see, think, move and barely breathe; to my family, for being my legs when I couldn't stand and to those that have breathed life back into me, at various times in my life, without realizing it…Anthony Clayton (RIP), Abdul Soudan, Geneva McCullough, Camille Brown, Pete Williams, Eric Lampkin, Stephan Thompson and Alanna Jones.

Contents

Introduction 9
Recovery 12
Answered Prayer 16
Ask 20
Be Confident 23
Be You 26
Believe Again 29
Believe What You Say 33
(Your) Business is God's Business 36
Called To Be 39
Choices 43
Deal With It 46
Decide 49
Destiny Defined 52
Embrace Today 55
Expectation 58
Faith 61
Feel 65
Flow of Life 68
Go Through It 72
Good to Forget 75
Growth 78

Healing 83

Heart of the Matter 86

Honesty 89

Hope 92

Inspire 95

Learn the Lesson 99

Let Go 102

Life is Waiting 105

Live 108

Love 111

Love & Wisdom 114

Love Yourself 117

Move Forward 120

Passion 123

The Past is the Past 127

Positive Attraction 131

Reality 134

Release 137

Remember 140

Rooted & Grounded 143

Seeds of Doubt 146

Start New 148

Storms 152

Take Time Out 156

Time 159
Trust Yourself 162
Venture Out 165
Vision 168
What 172
Who Are You 175
Who Said? 178
Words 181
Your Future 184
God is There 186

Introduction

The unexpected is one of the very few guarantees in life. One minute we are moving right along, living and loving life and the next minute something happens that causes a major interruption to life as we know it. It can leave us feeling lost, hurt, confused and even destroyed. Before long we are left wondering why we feel depleted and how we got to the point where all our energy and excitement for life have disappeared. I have been there and the only word that I can use to describe what I felt is numb. I needed hope, I needed something to revive me, something that would help me pick myself up and push me forward.

In difficult times, it's hard to find a lifeline to help you, let alone save you. During the difficult times I experienced, I learned the value of looking deep within myself for answers to the questions that at the time I couldn't understand nor fathom having the answers to. I learned the true power in prayer and that there is strength buried deep within me that I didn't know was there, because I never had to tap into it until something happened that forced me to. I believe that we all have exactly what we need within us, to survive. We just need a reminder of who we really are to pull it out of us. More times than not, that reminder has to come from none other than the one looking back at us in the mirror.

As hard as it may be, we have to both allow and demand the strength that resides on the inside of us to rise up and push us forward when everything around us is pulling us back. The times when you feel like giving up, are the times when you must push yourself harder.

I often hear in movies about the moments in life that take our breath away, but what about the moments when we need life breathed back into us. What do we do with the moments when we can't think straight, or in the moments that follow stress, struggle, loss, failure or heartbreak? What about the moments when we can't seem to catch a break when a break is all that we need? Sometimes a hint of inspiration, a kind word, or a touch from God is all that we need to remind us that our current circumstances don't define us, but it is we who define ourselves. We are the ones that must decide to get up after a fall; and we are the ones who decide that a fall doesn't equal failure, but that staying down after the fall very well could if we let it.

My prayer is that, as you reflect on these words; they inspire you, touch you, move you, awaken you, revive you and breathe life back into those areas where doubt and fear have overwhelmed your sense of reality; and give you back the desire to really live the life that you were created to live.

This book is designed for you to read, affirm and reflect. Read the message, speak the affirmation out loud and then take time to reflect on the meaning and journal any thoughts that come to mind.

What do you need to do, what do you have to do, what can you do right now, to recover and move forward?

Sometimes to begin again, you must first recover from what you've gone through.

What do you do when a life changing event happens in your life? What do you do when your world has changed and your earth is shattered? What do you do when your spirit is broken, your money is gone, your confidence is stripped, your mind is lost and you realize that the only bit of strength you have left is weak? What do you do when the world around you that was once full of life, full of friends, full of family, full of laughter and love is now silent? What do you do when the one you love, loves someone else; when the one who said they loved you left; when the relationship that you thought you had, never really was? What do you do when your innocence is taken, when you or someone you love is violated, when the hurt goes so deep that all you see, feel, hear and think is anger? What do you do when no words will comfort, no prayer brings you peace and no offered hand can help?

What do you do when your world has stopped, but no one else got the memo? What do you do when hours, days, weeks and months pass and it seems like you're still in the same moment?

What do you do when life is passing you by while you're stuck in your pain, in your grief, in your hurt, in your anger and in your frustrations?

No one can understand your pain the way that you do, because it's yours. No one can feel what you feel or see what you see or think how you think about what it is that you have experienced in your life. As unfair and as painful as what has happened in your life was, it can't be changed. So what do you do, to move forward?

You have to invite yourself to breathe, invite yourself to believe, invite yourself to get up, put one foot in front of the other and live again. Taking that first step, whatever it entails for you, toward recovery will take you from the pain you may be living in right now, to what your future can and should be. It won't be easy, but it is possible. You may have to take it one minute, hour or day at a time, and that's okay. Do whatever it is that you need to do, however you need to do it, at whatever pace you need to go, in order to get your healing and start moving through life again.

That's not to say that you won't still feel the void that was left by what or who you lost, or by what or who was taken from you; but by choosing to give yourself another chance you are choosing to live again. If by some chance when you take that first step, you discover that you're not ready yet, that's perfectly okay. Just promise yourself that you will try again tomorrow and as many tomorrows as you need, to make that first step a successful one.

Affirm & Reflect

Affirmation

*I commit to do whatever it is that I need to
in order to heal, to be whole
and to fully recover*

Reflection

Journal your thoughts on 'Recovery'

_____

_____

_____

_____

_____

Why ask if you're not willing to wait for the answer? Don't give up too soon.

You just might be one breath, one blink, one second, one thought, one person or one praise away from an answered prayer. Don't you dare give up now!

How many times have you almost given up? We all get to that point; the point when you throw your hands up in the air and just say "forget it!". It's not always easy to wait, when we want what we want or need what we need, right now. The next time that you want to give up, think about all of the time that you have spent praying, believing, confessing, sacrificing and standing firm in your faith for something that you wanted. Don't let that be wasted time. Think of it this way; if you were walking down the street to your dream car (keys in hand) and you knew that all you had to do was keep walking, turn right and it would be right there, would you stop walking, turn around and go the other way? Of course not! The answer to your prayers is there, possibly just a few steps away. Don't give up!

Affirm & Reflect

Affirmation

> *I believe that before I ask,*
> *God knows my thoughts,*
> *God hears my heart and*
> *God answers my prayers*

Reflection

Journal your thoughts on 'Answered Prayer'

_____

_____

_____

_____

_____

_____

Imagine how you will feel when you are standing in the middle of answered prayer.

> *If you need help, ask. You don't have to suffer in silence.*

It's okay to ask for help if & when you need it.

In the pain and frustration of what we may be going through and experiencing, we can get so caught up in that, sometimes we just expect for the people closest to us to be there and offer help. Even though we may want them to be, and it would be nice if they were, people are not mind readers. We can't assume that they just know what we are going through and what we need help with. We can't let pride, embarrassment, shame, doubt, hesitation or fear keep us from reaching out to a family member, a friend, our church or possibly even to someone who we don't know. At some point in our lives, we all need help. There is someone or some organization that can and will lend a helping hand…our job is to ask and to ask until we get what it is we need.

You never know who God has assigned to be right there, at your exact moment of need.

Affirm & Reflect

Affirmation

*Asking for help does not make me weak.
When I need help, I will ask for it
with my head held high and
my dignity intact.*

Reflection

Journal your thoughts on 'Ask'

_____

_____

_____

_____

_____

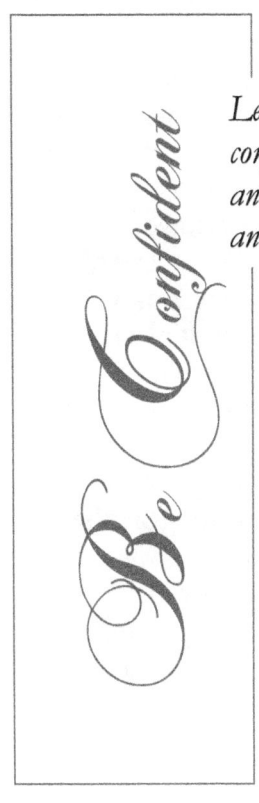

Let nothing impact your confidence. Face the world and everything in it boldly and with confidence!

What we think of ourselves, is a reflection to others.

Just as confidence shows, so does the lack thereof. We all have times in life, when we second guess ourselves. There are some situations we've been in, that when we look back, we wish we would have handled differently. Maybe it was a conversation in which we didn't respond the way we wish we would have, because the right thoughts came to mind after the fact instead of at that moment. Or maybe it is something that we've done, that we wish we could go back and do over again and have a better result. Whatever it was, we can't let the moments that have passed; those moments that we can do nothing about, impact our confidence now. If we keep reliving times when we felt defeated, we will always feel like we are defeated. Have you ever noticed that when you think about a situation, whether it be happy or sad, you feel the same emotions that you felt when it was actually happening? Reliving moments of defeat, will keep you in the feelings that you experienced in those moments.

There will be other opportunities, providing another chance to react exactly the way we should, when we should. The moral to the story is that we can't let what we did or didn't do in a particular situation in the past, impact the strength of who we are today or who it is we will become tomorrow. What we think about ourselves is reflected on the outside in our attitude and our actions. Always exude confidence.

Affirm & Reflect

Affirmation

*Regardless of past
disappointments or failures,
I am confident and secure in
who I am.*

Reflection

Journal your thoughts on 'Be Confident'

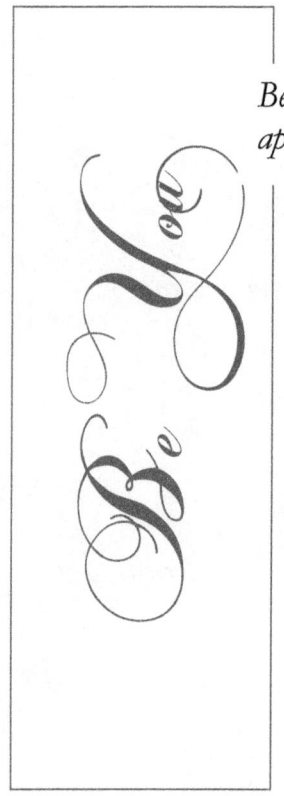

Be uniquely you, with no apologies.

Stand up tall, be who you are and speak YOUR truth.

There are some people who will try whatever method they can to shrink you into what they want you to be or what's comfortable for them. Don't ever allow anyone to put you in a box. Don't ever allow anyone to cause you to question or doubt who you are. Don't ever allow someone to make you feel small in order to make themselves appear "big" or better about whatever it is they have going on internally. Someone trying to control what you have to express and how you express it, is someone who has issues. The issue is not with you, know that.

The world is full of enough "cookie cutter" people. Those are people who follow instead of lead, who look, talk and act like the images they see, instead of being original. They go with the flow in order to fit in with crowd. Don't be one of those people.

Be YOU, standing tall and standing strong!

Affirm & Reflect

Affirmation

*I am fearfully, wonderfully
and beautifully made.
I am uniquely me and that is
more than enough.*

Reflection

Journal your thoughts on 'Be You'

_____

_____

_____

_____

_____

_____

The only way that you stop believing is if YOU stop believing. The choice is yours…

Love again, try again, touch again, feel again, begin again and believe again.

Dreams, hopes and desires deferred can leave you feeling disappointed. Sometimes, so much so, that you stop believing. Enough bad experiences, and sometimes even one, can leave you asking "what's the purpose in believing in something that just isn't going to happen for me". Experiences come to teach us something and I know that it's hard to understand that or think that way, in the middle of disappointment. The feelings that remained after whatever happened, whatever hurt and disappointed you, weren't meant to last forever. You may have been left feeling like every ounce of faith that you had in you was stripped, but please know that as long as you still have breath in your body, you have something to offer, to live for, to once again believe in.

You have a life to live, you have strength within you to give, you have a well of knowledge to share and experience that will change a life and maybe even help someone survive. Make the choice to believe again, there's still hope.

Affirm & Reflect

Affirmation

*In the face of adversity,
in the midst of trials
and in the heart of hurt,
I will choose to believe.*

Reflection

Journal your thoughts on 'Believe Again'

Believe that it will be okay and that all will be well.

Believe What You Say

What carries more weight with you...what other people say about you or what you say about yourself?

What someone else says about you is not your truth.

Most of us grew up either being teased or teasing others. If you were teased, sometimes those words, hurt feelings, humiliation and embarrassment surface in the present and cause you to feel the same way that you felt then. People will always have something to say. In someone else's mind you will always be too much or not enough, in some way. But who cares what someone else has to say? What do you have to say about yourself? What positive words do you speak about yourself? What positive things do you speak into your life? That's what matters. Just because someone says and maybe even believes something about you, doesn't make it true. What matters is what you believe about yourself. The words that **you** speak set the foundation for **your life**. Speak what you want to see even if it's not true yet and believe that it can be exactly as you have spoken it.

Words are powerful! So make the ones that you speak about and over yourself positive, bold, confident and strong.

Affirm & Reflect

Affirmation

*I speak truth & light
into my life
and it will be so*

Reflection

Journal your thoughts on 'Believe Again'

_____

_____

_____

_____

_____

_____

Pray, believe, confess, do your part and watch God take care of the rest.

God will take care of you.

Let me share a little bit with you about the business that God is in.

God is in the suddenly business!
God is in the blessing business!
God is in the restoring business!
God is in the healing business!
God is in the protecting business!
God is in the business of giving you the desires of your heart!
God is in the business of re-birthing the dreams and desires of your heart!
God is in the business of redeeming the time.

Your desires, your heart, your health, your family, your time, your dreams are all God's business and He will take care of them. Your job is to trust & believe.

Affirm & Reflect

Affirmation

*God will take care of me.
My faith
in Him will not waiver.*

Reflection

Journal your thoughts on 'Your Business is God's Business'

What is your passion? What touches your heart? What moves your emotions? What really drives you? Somewhere in there lies your calling.

You are here to do something unique, something that no one else can do the way that you can.

Most people get an inkling of what their calling is early in life. I have been keeping journals and writing stories since the third grade. I love to write and to touch the hearts of people, to uplift, motivate, inspire and change lives through words, that is my calling. Although I work in corporate America full-time, that is not my calling, it is simply my job. There are things that I like to do, such as community service and volunteer work. While those are things that I like to do, those things are not my calling. I know what and who I was called to be. Let me encourage you today, if you don't already know what you are called to do, find out. Once you know, follow that and don't waste time trying to do anything else. Sometimes people will try to keep you where they want you to be because you are helping them to fulfill their calling. Don't get so busy helping someone else with their vision that you don't have time to work toward your own. You have a specific calling, you are here to do something that only you can do. Don't leave this world without doing it.

Life has a way of getting in the way, so to speak. No matter how long it takes you to get in position to pursue your calling, the important thing is that you do it. It is never too late to be what you were called to be.

Affirm & Reflect

Affirmation

*In my calling
is where I find fulfillment.
I will do what I am called to do
and be who I am called to be.*

Reflection

Journal your thoughts on 'Called to Be'

_____

_____

_____

_____

_____

If you just hold on for another second, another minute, another hour, another day...you will give yourself another chance to try again. You deserve that.

Make the relationship choices that are best for you.

Whatever is in your best interest…choose that.

We have all heard it said time and time again, in many different ways by several different people; when someone shows you EXACTLY who they are, believe them. The important thing is what you do with that information once it's handed to you. You can choose to keep the people in your life that are full of drama and negativity or you can choose to remove them. But before you make the decision, ask yourself why you stay in any type of relationship with someone that abuses you in any form or fashion? I mean from the smallest form of abuse, to the largest. Why would you tolerate and defend someone who lies to you, cheats you, mistreats you or uses you? Why would you want to be in a relationship with someone who is self-centered and self-righteous and behind all that selfishness, you have simply become an afterthought? Why wouldn't you put yourself first? Why wouldn't you choose yourself, your happiness, your well-being and your life, over that?

People have the option to act a straight fool if they want to (and they definitely will if you let them), but that doesn't mean that you have to stick around for it. Choose you!

Affirm & Reflect

Affirmation

I choose me!

Reflection

Journal your thoughts on 'Choices'

___

___

___

___

___

Trying to avoid what life hands to you just simply doesn't work; however dealing with it does.

Sometimes in life it becomes necessary to just sit still and deal.

Stop running from yourself and stop running from what you have never dealt with. What you don't realize is that all the running is simply holding you back from being who that situation can help you grow into. There are unspeakable things that happen to people in life and while I have suffered through some very hurtful experiences, I know that what I've experienced doesn't touch the surface of what others have been through. When we deal with the rough, tough, hard and difficult things that happen to us in life, they help us to grow and mature. We are all different and in turn deal with pain differently. Sometimes we have to reach within ourselves, reach up to God or reach out to others to help us heal. If we do not do what is necessary to heal, we won't grow or be able to thrive in life. Allow that situation to turn you into a person of passion, motivated to help others get over their fear and past their pain.

Don't cover up or mask "it" any longer. Deal with it, address it, respond to it, face it, get delivered from it and move on to living a good life and helping others live the life that they were meant to live. *There is a mentor, motivator and minister inside of you.*

Affirm & Reflect

Affirmation

*I face challenges head on.
I receive my
healing, by dealing!*

Reflection

Journal your thoughts on 'Deal With It'

_____

_____

_____

_____

_____

This is your life, so let your decisions get you through it, not someone else's.

Stop second guessing yourself and make the decision.

Decide what's best for you right now, and make that the final say. Too often we seek the advice of others, when what we are really looking for is someone to validate what we already know. Somewhere along the way we learned that we should get confirmation from other people before we make a move. Who knows what you need to do for you, better than you? You have more inside information, on your life, your situations and your circumstances, than anyone you know. Stop waiting on other people to tell you how to live, act and be. This is your life and you only get one, so live it for you. Start learning to trust yourself and your decisions, after all you're the most qualified to make them.

Affirm & Reflect

Affirmation

*I will not procrastinate.
I will make the decision when
it needs to be made. <u>I will</u>
take action for myself & my life.*

Reflection

Journal your thoughts on 'Decide'

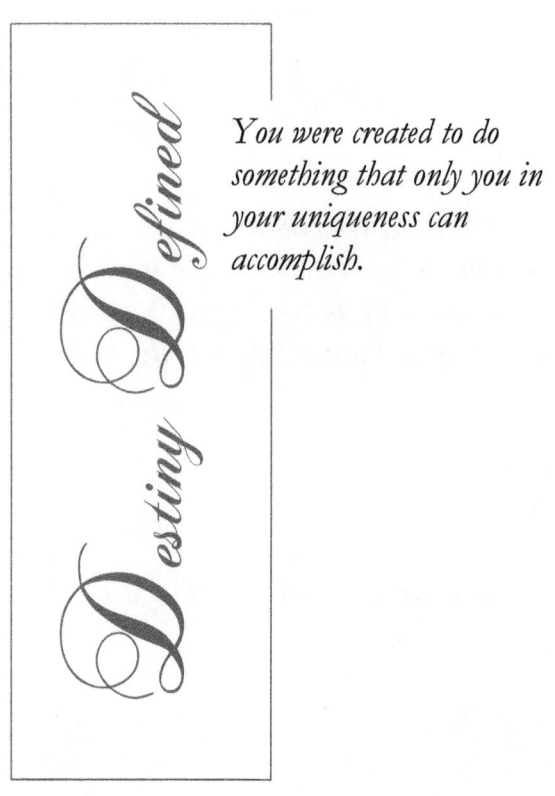

Destiny Defined

You were created to do something that only you in your uniqueness can accomplish.

Your destiny is waiting for you to arrive.

Do you ever have the feeling that there is something greater out there waiting for you or that you could be doing so much more than what you are doing now? Do you ever think that you could be impacting so many more people than you already have or that you have something in you that could change the world, or at least a piece of it? Do you ever have glimpses of your future? Do you just have a knowing that where you are now is not where you will be, when you finally reach your destiny? Well, you are right!! That feeling, the desire to do or be something more and the glimpses of your future are all pushing you toward your destiny.

I believe that every person and every creation was made for a specific purpose and that purpose was defined before we ever arrived on the scene. If you don't already know what that specific purpose is for you, find out and start moving toward your destiny. The sooner you start, the sooner you'll get there. What better life to live, than the one that you were destined for.

Affirm & Reflect

Affirmation

*I will cross the bridge
that connects me to
my destiny.*

Reflection

Journal your thoughts on 'Destiny Defined'

_____

_____

_____

_____

_____

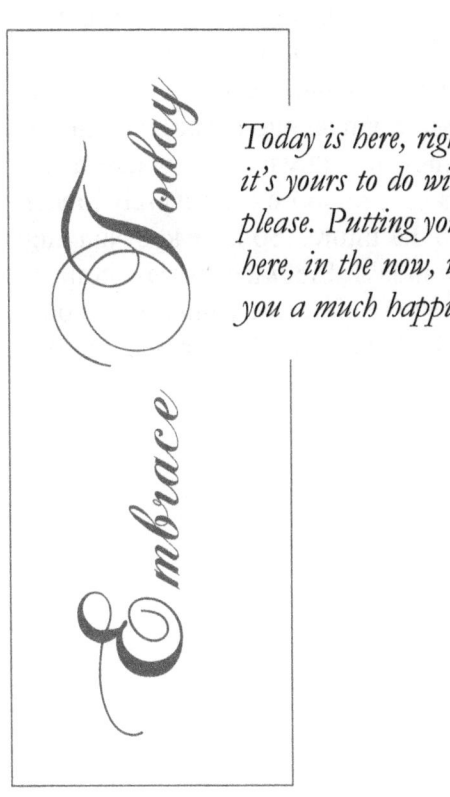

Today is here, right now and it's yours to do with as you please. Putting your focus here, in the now, will make you a much happier person.

Don't get stuck on yesterday. Release it, let it be what it was and move on. Today is here now, embrace that.

The easiest way to keep from moving forward is by continuously looking back. We love people, we lose people, we hurt, we heal, the present becomes the past and the cycle of life goes on. It's dangerous to get so wrapped up in the past that you forget to live in the present or become closed to the opportunities of the future. It's nice to take a stroll down memory lane from time to time. It holds laughter, love and beautiful memories that can never and should never be replaced. But getting stuck somewhere down memory lane and longing for things that are no more can severely hinder your progress toward the future. So instead of longing for the past, embrace today! Embrace the day, hour, minute and second that is before you right now. You can own that and make it exactly what you want it to be.

Affirm & Reflect

Affirmation

*The past is the past, I can't change it.
But there is plenty that I can do about
today and even more that I can
do about tomorrow.*

Reflection

Journal your thoughts on 'Embrace Today'

_____

_____

_____

_____

_____

Expectation

Since waiting for the future isn't optional, why not wait with expectation.

Waiting isn't so bad when you have an expected end.

In life, we are always waiting. There is always the thought of what will come next, what's waiting around the corner, what's down the road or the thought that there has to be something more than "this". As we wait, we are still living, being, breathing, moving, doing and working toward whatever is next. There is a difference in just waiting and waiting for something with expectation. What do you expect to be waiting for you in the end? Do you just wait for tomorrow to arrive and that's it or do you wait for tomorrow with the expectation that it will be better than today, that you will accomplish more, believe more, dream bigger, laugh louder, set goals, accomplish those goals, set your vision and see that vision come to pass. What are you expecting to be next, to be around the corner or down the road for you? Sometimes waiting can be frustrating but when you have an expected outcome and you actively work toward it, waiting becomes worth it in the end.

Affirm & Reflect

Affirmation

*I live life expecting
the next "thing", to be
better than the last and for my
future to be greater than my past!*

Reflection

Journal your thoughts on 'Expectation'

In the face of adversity, fear and doubt... choose faith!

Sometimes having faith isn't easy.

There are times when it seems like if there is room for something else to go wrong, it will. Just when you save money, your car needs a major repair or just when you decide to take a vacation, the furnace in your house goes out. Just when you think that you can finally get ahead, you get knocked back 10 steps. All faith counts, but I tend to think that the faith that really, really counts is the faith that you have when all hell has seemingly broken loose against you. When you are hit hard on every side and you still believe that in the end everything will work out just fine, that's faith. When you determine to get up, even when you get knocked down time and time again; God, the universe and life can't help but to respond to faith like that.

No matter how hard it's been for you, continue to believe, continue moving forward. In the face of worry, doubt and fear...have faith!

Affirm & Reflect

Affirmation

*No matter what comes against me,
my faith will stand!
My faith will be my anchor!
My faith will see me through.*

Reflection

Journal your thoughts on 'Faith'

Regardless of who you are or what you have achieved, when it is time for a lesson to be learned, life will deliver it to you. Be encouraged & know that your *Faith* will carry you through that season in your life.

Don't hide it, mask it or cover it up...allow yourself to feel what you feel.

If no one else has ever told you, I'm telling you that it is okay to feel what you feel, at the moment you feel it.

At some point in life, whether it is what our parents taught us, what school taught us, what society taught us or what life lessons taught us; somewhere along the way we learned that we need to hide our feelings. That we need to dismiss them, bottle them up or suppress them on the inside. I wonder how many people were ever taught to actually deal with what they were feeling at the moment they feel it. What would happen if when we got hurt, we admitted to being hurt instead of masking it in anger and building walls in order to protect ourselves? There are a lot of wounded people walking around this earth because they never dealt with what they were feeling, WHEN they were feeling it.

You have to feel it, digest it, understand it and then release it. It will not do you, your friends, your spouse, your kids, your parents, your co-workers or anyone else in your life any good for you to walk around with bottled up feelings on the inside. When you keep bottling and keep bottling and keep bottling your feelings, it is a great possibility that eventually they will explode in the wrong way, toward the wrong person, at the wrong time. A*llow* yourself to feel whatever it is that you are feeling, address it and then let it go.

Affirm & Reflect

Affirmation

*For my benefit and the benefit of
those I love,
I will address what I feel, when I feel it.*

Reflection

Journal your thoughts on 'Feel'

_____

_____

_____

_____

_____

Think of life as a rhythm, some up beats and some down; but learning to flow with them all.

Flow with the rhythms of life...

In order to flow in life you have to be free. Free from the judgments that others place on you and those that you place on yourself. Free from the criticisms of others and from your own. Once you are truly free, you will thrive. I once heard someone talk about what they do under pressure. Instead of tensing up and fighting against the grain or fighting against whatever is happening, they said that they become fluid, like liquid, able to move and flow with the situation and eventually they flow right on over it and into whatever is next. That's how we should all be.

If you've lived any amount of time on this earth, you know that life will throw unexpected blows your way. It seems like it happens more often than not. We can't escape the things that happen to us or having to deal with what comes our way, but we should learn to flow with what comes. Fighting against life's pressures can bring unnecessary stress, anger and frustration and those are all things we can do without.

Affirm & Reflect

Affirmation

*I ebb and flow with
the tides of life.
I am fluid under pressure
and move as such.*

Reflection

Journal your thoughts on 'Flow of Life'

_____

_____

_____

_____

_____

_____

Think about how much easier life would be if you got in the right groove and simply started to flow

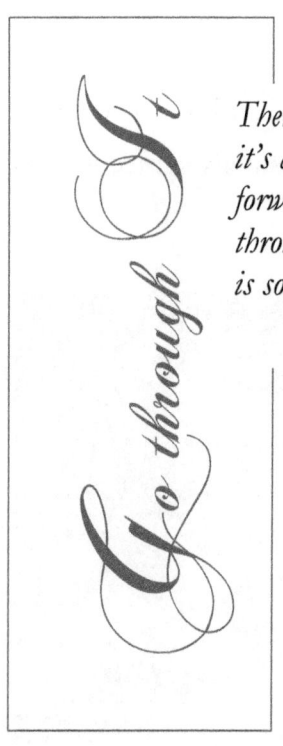

There is a theme forming and it's all about movement. Move forward, keep going, and go through it...that's because there is something waiting for you.

Have Faith, Believe, Find Peace & Breathe

It will be okay. Remember, when you are going through something, the key is to *go through it* and be determined to come out on the other side stronger and better than when you went in. The problem usually comes in when we decide to stay in a place that we were meant to go through and grow through. Trials come to make us stronger. If we give up before we get through the trial, we lose the opportunity to get the strength that the experience was designed to give us. Don't setup camp in the middle of the mess. Grab the lesson and move on.

Affirm & Reflect

Affirmation

> *I grab hold of
> life's lessons
> and move forward.*

Reflection

Journal your thoughts on 'Go Through It'

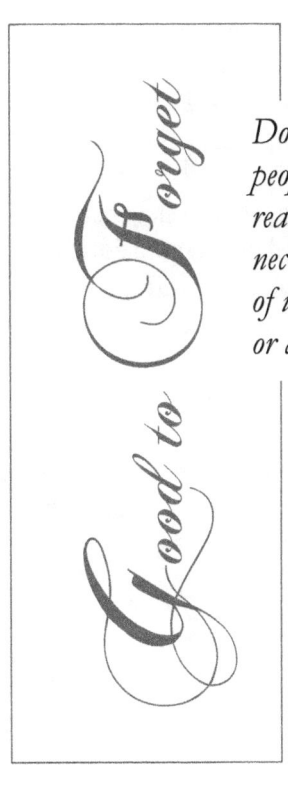

Don't be afraid to leave people and places behind to reach the next level. It is a necessary step in life that all of us must take, at one point or another.

Sometimes you have to forget the good ole days, to move on to the better ones that lie ahead.

There are people, who have been toxic to our lives; who have hurt us to the core of our beings. There are situations that we have been in, that have fed certain addictions or addictive behavior that we have struggled to get free of. When those same people attempt to come back into our lives or when those situations present themselves to us again, there are some things that we need to consider and others that we need to remember. While we may have had good times with those people and in those situations, there is a reason that we got away from, and out of them. If there is a time for us to forget the good times and remember the bad or maybe I should say, remember the consequences of what was disguised as good, but really did us harm in the end; it is at that moment when those situations or people show up again. It's good to forget, if it will keep us from making the same mistake for a second, third or fourth time. We need to remember the reason we gave the invitation for the person or situation to exit our lives in the first place and make that the reason that they are not invited back in.

Affirm & Reflect

Affirmation

> *I will not go back
> to anything or anyone
> that was toxic
> to my life.*

Reflection

Journal your thoughts on 'Good to Forget'

When you look back over your life, can you see how you've grown over time or is what you see the same, year after year?

Don't let your doubts turn into fears and stunt your growth.

We all have doubts, but we cannot allow our doubts to stay there so long that they turn into fears. Fear, if not dealt with, will take root in us and cause us to become indecisive. Fear will stop us in our tracks and we can end up just standing still in life; not moving, not changing, not growing and not truly being who it is we were meant to be. One of the worst feelings in life is being stagnant when you know on the inside that you should be growing and reaching higher heights but fear has taken hold of you and rendered you helpless. Fear takes the smallest concern, magnifies it and turns it into a major life issue, when it really isn't. Get rid of doubt, face your fears head on and I guarantee that they will dissipate right before your eyes.

If you are in the same place year after year, and that is not your true desire or intent, it could be that fear is stopping you. The good news is that you can change that.

Affirm & Reflect

Affirmation

*I allow myself to grow
by facing my
fears.*

Reflection

Journal your thoughts on 'Growth'

Instead of focusing on what other people want you to do, be and say, focus on the things that truly make you *Happy*.

Just be...

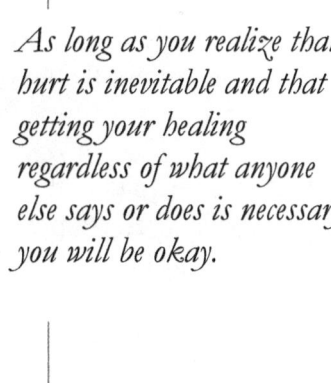

As long as you realize that hurt is inevitable and that getting your healing regardless of what anyone else says or does is necessary, you will be okay.

Wholeness and healing are yours for the taking.

Remember that hurting people, hurt people. There may have been someone in your life that said or did something to you, that broke your spirit. Most times it doesn't matter how long ago it happened, because if you continuously relive it in your mind it seems like it just happened. The emotions stay fresh and the hurt remains raw. It would be nice if all the people that ever wronged us, realized the error of their ways and came back and apologized to give us closure. Unfortunately that is just not the way that it happens for most of us.

Understand that most people do the best that they can. I have always thought when people said "they don't know any better" was just an excuse, but in some cases that's true. People don't always know how to address situations or leave situations tactfully so they take the easy way out and while that way is easier on them, it usually leaves the other person or people involved hurt. Just know that the hurt you experienced has very little to do with you and everything to do with them. It wasn't your fault. That's why it is important to learn to release it and let it go on your own without looking to the one who hurt you. You owe yourself the whole and healed you.

Affirm & Reflect

Affirmation

*I do not depend on
outside sources for the health of my
emotions. I release the
pains of the past so that I can be free.*

Reflection

Journal your thoughts on 'Healing'

___

___

___

___

___

___

Heart of the Matter

Dig deep and find out what's going on within you, them, the situation or the circumstance before you act.

Before you act, move or decide; get to the heart of the matter.

In the heat of an argument, in the middle of a crisis, in the depths of depression, in the height of dysfunction or in the fresh hurt of a broken heart is not the time to make a permanent decision or change in your life. In some situations we are required to make quick decisions, sometimes for the sake of our survival and sanity. But before you make a permanent life decision take a step back, take some time to breathe, to digest what's really happening in and around you and then move. What we see on the surface is not always what's at the core. You never want to make a permanent decision based on a temporary circumstance. Making "snap" decisions comes as second nature to most people. Something happens and there's an immediate reaction. Relationships end, business ties sever and people end up with bruised emotions over something that should have never been said or done.

When emotions are running high, take a step back and make a conscious decision to let the smoke clear, allow the dust to settle and then act.

Affirm & Reflect

Affirmation

I will pause before I act so that my actions are not just an emotional response, but a genuine reaction to the reality of my situation.

Reflection

Journal your thoughts on 'Heart of the Matter'

_____

_____

_____

_____

_____

_____

Most people see the reality of who we are, behind the pretenses and the protections that we've placed around us.

It's time to get honest, not with them, but with you...

When someone tells you about yourself, how do you react? Do you hear them or do you get defensive and start making passive aggressive remarks? Do you respond with sarcasm? Do you try to make it about their issues, just to ignore the fact that you have just been called out on yours? Do you get up and walk away saying; "I don't have time for this"? How do you respond and why do you respond that way? In order to have a healthy, whole relationship, not only with others but also with yourself, you have to learn how to be honest with yourself first. Instead of getting defensive or shutting down, listen and become open when someone makes the effort to talk to you about their perception of you and your actions, in an open and honest way. You just might learn something about yourself that you didn't realize or maybe you realized but didn't want to face. Open and honest communication, on both the giving and receiving end, creates an environment of trust and comfort. Give that to those you love and give that to yourself.

Affirm & Reflect

Affirmation

*I am open and willing
to receive honest
communication about myself
from others.*

Reflection

Journal your thoughts on 'Honesty'

If you lose hope, there isn't much left. Regardless of what and who comes up against you, hold on to hope.

Hold on to your hope...

Don't let someone else's actions or opinions deter or defer YOUR hope. There will always be certain people in life that will try to discourage you, to bring you down, to interrupt you on your journey to reaching your full potential and even some that will make every attempt to hurt or destroy you. Some of them, if not most of them will come in disguise, as someone that cares, loves and supports you. Watch out for those that little by little start to chip away at your hope. There are some people who see in you, what they are lacking in themselves, and those people will admire it and strive to obtain it too. And then there are those whose envy will try to steal it from you. Don't let someone else rob you of the fuel that keeps your fire lit. No matter what it seems like, looks like, or feels like...hold on to your hope!

Against hope...believe in hope. *Romans 4:18*

Affirm & Reflect

Affirmation

*Against hope,
I believe in hope.
I will walk by faith
no matter what I see or feel*

Reflection

Journal your thoughts on 'Hope'

> *Inspiring yourself will help inspire those around you. You will help them feel the fire and catch the flame.*

Inspire

What inspires you? What motivates you?

If you have yet to discover what really inspires you, take some time to find out and then surround yourself with those things. This world is full of so much beauty and so much to learn. Forget the world; the city you live in is full of something that can inspire you.

Whether it be the museums, the parks, the drive of the people, the graffiti, or the architecture, I bet that there is something right where you are that can bring a fresh flow of inspiration into your life. So often we get stuck in a routine or two in life and forget that there is so much more around us to see and to do. Sometimes the emptiness that we feel on the inside is because we've forgotten that there is so much around us that can inspire us and our world has become limited to just the things that fit into our routines.

It's time to color outside of the lines. Go exploring and find that inspiration and zest for life again.

Affirm & Reflect

Affirmation

*I am inspired by the things
that surround me.
I am inspired
by Life!*

Reflection

Journal your thoughts on 'Inspire'

Let *Life* be your inspiration

Life happens and when it does it can hurt, but we have to take away from the experience whatever was meant for us to learn.

Learning the lesson is not always the easiest thing to do.

When you put your emotions to the side, step away from trying to understand, from being upset and make the decision to just be. That is when you will learn the lesson. We go through so many things in life that we do not and in some cases, will not ever understand. We go through things that we never thought we would go through and most of them hit us out of nowhere. One minute we are moving along in life just fine and the next we are suffering loss, sickness or facing something so unexpected that we don't know what to do or how to do it. Sometimes the pain can be so unbearable, we become broken. We don't see the purpose, the reason or the sense in any of it and most times there is no sense, reason or purpose. But one thing I do know is that God will use those situations for a purpose. He will use them to stretch you, to get you out of your comfort zone, to push you into realizing a strength that you never knew you had. I know it's hard to do because I've been there time and time again, but as hard as it may be, we must focus on the lesson, not the experience. The lesson will teach you whatever it is you need to move to the next level in life. One certainty in life is that the unexpected will happen. With each lesson learned comes the opportunity to handle the next challenge with more ease and wisdom than the time before it. Within every painful experience lies a lesson; take the time to learn it. You'll need it later in life.

Affirm & Reflect

Affirmation

*Instead of rushing through
and past situations in life;
I will take the time
that I need to learn the lesson.*

Reflection

Journal your thoughts on 'Learn the Lesson'

It's not healthy to hold on when you've already lost your grip. Let go.

Letting go releases not only that person or thing that you are holding on to, but it also releases you.

We've all had experiences in life that caused us to hold on to something or someone too long. Maybe it was a relationship that was over, a job that we no longer fit or that no longer fit us, a position in life that we no longer held or a family member that made their transition. There are things and people who we hold on to that have already left us. Holding on for dear life can blind us from realizing that our grip has already been lost, and it or they are gone. We have to be careful holding on to things that are lost, situations that have passed or to people that have moved on. Remember the very thing that we are holding on to can be the thing that is responsible for holding us back. Don't get stuck somewhere that you weren't meant to stay. Remembering is natural and healthy, holding on can be just the opposite. We have to realize when something has run its course; it's time for us to let it go. There is something else for you, but it can't come until you learn to let go of the old and make room for the new.

Affirm & Reflect

Affirmation

*In order to move forward,
I let go of that
which has served it's
purpose in my life.*

Reflection

Journal your thoughts on 'Let Go'

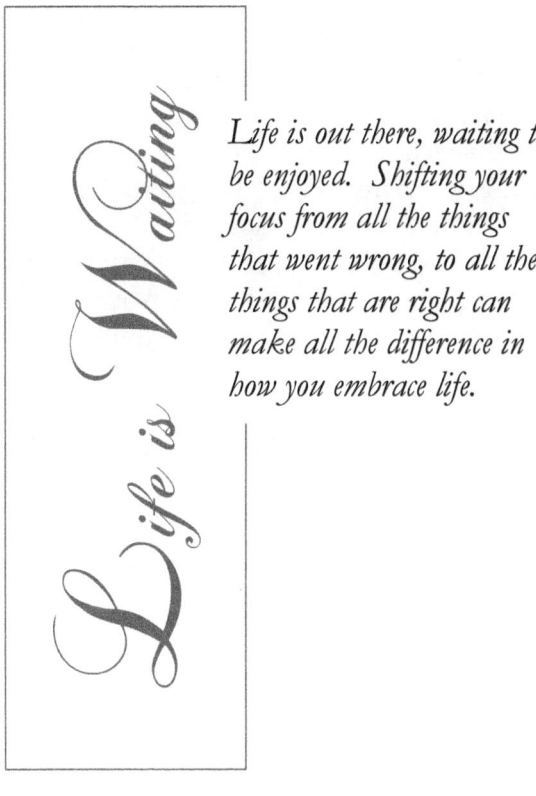

Life is Waiting

Life is out there, waiting to be enjoyed. Shifting your focus from all the things that went wrong, to all the things that are right can make all the difference in how you embrace life.

Live, I mean really <u>live</u> your life!

Don't miss out on life waiting on wounds to heal, people to change, your bank account to grow, until you lose weight, until you gain weight, until you get older or any of the many other reasons we put off *really* living. I can't tell you how much of my life I have wasted being sad, broken-hearted, frustrated, angry and just plain old broken; body, mind and spirit. I lost time precious time that I could have spent enjoying life, loving those who cared enough to stick around, being grateful for the things and people who I was blessed to have in my life, being thankful for having a roof over my head (even during the times when I didn't have one of my own), clothes on my back and food on my table. Life is not what happens to you. What life, your life becomes, is determined by the outlook that you have and what you choose to make of it.

Life is waiting for you...are you ready to live it? Then what are you waiting for? Life is ready and waiting with open arms.

Affirm & Reflect

Affirmation

*My outlook in life is positive,
no matter what happens.
I embrace life
and it will embrace me back!*

Reflection

Journal your thoughts on 'Life is Waiting'

_____

_____

_____

_____

_____

_____

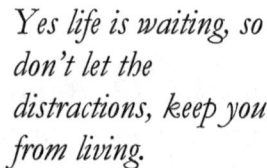
Yes life is waiting, so don't let the distractions, keep you from living.

There is no such thing as a distraction free life.

If you are living, breathing and walking on this earth, you have distractions coming at you from every which way. There are unexpected events at every turn, but you can't allow those distractions to stop you from doing, moving, enjoying and living. Distractions will always be there, but you can live without them causing major interference in your life. Every day that we wake up, is a new opportunity, to live life fully and freely. I believe that is what we all want, but worry, fear, stress, and hesitation all accompany the distractions and we end up focusing on them instead of living a full, free and happy life. If we would learn to stop over-thinking the distractions and stop giving them life by talking about them all the time, to whoever will listen, we would win half of the battle. Decide today, this very minute, that you will move past, over or around the distractions that come your way and live the life that you want to live.

Affirm & Reflect

Affirmation

*I deserve to be happy
and to live life
to the fullest &
I decide at this very moment
that I will!*

Reflection

Journal your thoughts on 'Live'

_____

_____

_____

_____

_____

> *Be open to the thought, idea and experience of real love.*

Love

Give yourself permission to experience real, unconditional, uninhibited love.

Being betrayed, taken advantage of, cheated on, lied to and treated in a way in which you did not in any way deserve, along with a list of many, many other things that can go wrong in what we think is a love relationship, can keep you from experiencing real love. The perception that a lot of people have of love, is based on an experience that was called love, but was anything but. There are even some people that believe love is supposed to hurt, because that's all they've ever known or been exposed to. Hear me and hear me clearly; love does not hurt!

Love heals, love purifies, love covers you, love protects you, love honors you, love supports you, love stands with you, love is honest, love is trustworthy, love is honorable, love makes you smile, feel free and breathe easy. If you haven't experienced that kind of love yet, become open to it and believe that it will find you.

Affirm & Reflect

Affirmation

*I throw out all
negative perceptions of
love from the past and become open
to experience genuine love.*

Reflection

Journal your thoughts on 'Love'

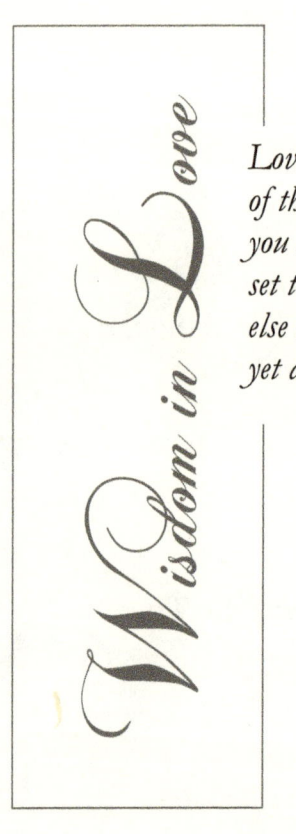

Wisdom in Love

Loving yourself first is one of the wisest decisions that you will ever make. It will set the tone for everything else that you allow, or better yet don't allow, in your life.

Know yourself well enough to know what & who is toxic to your life, and then get busy cleaning house.

If you notice certain things or people who drain your energy, exhaust your mind and grieve your spirit; get rid of them! This is probably one of the most important tasks that you could ever assign to yourself.

When we take on other people's issues, problems, drama and stress; if we allow it to, it can be toxic to OUR lives. We have the power to say NO, to say ENOUGH IS ENOUGH. Your life, your health, your environment, your overall well-being is your responsibility. Don't let someone else bring their mess into your world. People will rarely change and that's cool, they don't have to, but you can use and apply wisdom to know when it's time to change the role they play in your life or cut your association with them altogether. Love yourself enough to not only realize that you don't have to house someone else's drama in your life, but also enough to remove it from your life.

Affirm & Reflect

Affirmation

*I vow to keep my life,
my thoughts, my emotions and my
time clear of other people's
clutter.*

Reflection

Journal your thoughts on 'Wisdom in Love'

_____

_____

_____

_____

_____

_____

Yes, it's a love fest and it all begins and ends with you.

Go to a mirror, look yourself in the eyes and repeat after me…

"You are Beautiful and I Love You Just the Way you are".

Now sit in silence and reflect on what you just said and who you just said it to. Initially you may look away, you may even feel silly and the emotions or feelings that rise up on the inside of you when you say it, just might surprise you. As you reflect, you may realize that this is the first time that you've ever said I love you, to yourself. You might not feel comfortable, but keep saying it until you do, keep saying it until you really mean it. You loving yourself...really loving yourself, makes all the difference in the world. It makes a difference in your self-esteem, your interactions with others and your overall outlook. There is only one you! You are the only one created to do what you are called to do, the way that only you can do it. You are the only one shaped and molded into the beautiful being that you are. Learning to love yourself first, helps you learn to love everyone else fully & completely.

Affirm & Reflect

Affirmation

*I love myself
just the way I am*

Reflection

Journal your thoughts on 'Love Yourself'

_____

_____

_____

_____

_____

Move Forward

With every ounce of strength that you have in you, keep going!

Let the hard times catapult you into your next level in life.

Life happens. Most of our painful experiences are unexpected, undesired, unwanted and unwelcome. While they are all that were mentioned and sometimes much more, we can't let them destroy us. Instead we absolutely positively must draw strength from the pain and use it to move on to what's next for us in life. You have the power to decide whether something will or won't break you. You have the power to decide whether you will stand still or whether you will move forward in life. Choose to move forward and see what's waiting for you at the next turn.

Affirm & Reflect

Affirmation

> *I will move forward*
> *on my journey,*
> *regardless of what life*
> *throws in my path.*

Reflection

Journal your thoughts on 'Move Forward'

Passion

Don't go through this life without being passionate about and fully awakened to something.

Purpose today to live your life with passion; otherwise you'll just end up having a series of mediocre experiences. Life is so much more than that.

It's easy to get stagnant, to not move, or to move within a very small circumference. Go to work, school, church, and home and maybe pay a visit to a family member or a friend every now and then. Everything becomes routine and we do what we do, only because we feel like we have to. Life is so much more than just the routines that we've established within our comfort zones. Find passion in something. Do something or experience something that excites your senses! What is it that you love? What is it that makes you smile? What makes you feel alive? Explore that, do that, breathe that, *LIVE* that, and do it with passion!!

Affirm & Reflect

Affirmation

*I open my eyes,
breathe in life,
and embrace it with passion!*

Reflection

Journal your thoughts on 'Passion'

_____

_____

_____

_____

_____

A life lived without *Passion*, isn't really a life lived

The Past is the Past

Leave yesterday where it is and focus on today. Yesterday has already happened but today and tomorrow are ours to do with as we please!

Don't let your yesterdays kill your today or steal your tomorrows; instead learn from yesterday, live today and promise yourself a better tomorrow.

The past is the past and you have to learn to leave it there. That is often easier said than done. Things that have happened in the past hurt us; left parts of us destroyed and may have even deterred our destiny. Some of those things left our souls bruised, our minds blank and our hearts broken. Things that happened in the past, if we want to be honest, have hurt our egos, made us question our faith, have left us wondering if we really knew what we thought we did and at the end of the day, have left us wondering WHY. Sometimes all the wondering and questioning in the world will never bring us the answers that we are seeking. Sometimes you and I just have to simply let it go and not let what happened yesterday, keep us from living today.

Whatever it was, leave it back there where it belongs. Focus on what you can do something about, that's the here and now.

Affirm & Reflect

Affirmation

*I will not allow
my past to steal my faith,
my energy or
my life, I let it go.*

Reflection

Journal your thoughts on 'The Past is the Past'

_____

_____

_____

_____

_____

The world is in a rush but you don't have to be. Slow down, be *Patient* and be sure not to miss what's for you, by rushing past it.

Positive Attraction

Draw to you, that which you desire, with your thoughts, words, attitude and vibrations. Be & think positive.

Changing your outlook, will change your life.

The things that many of us have been through and suffered in life, make it easy to think negative thoughts. We have become angry, bitter and frustrated. Even though we want to move past the bad experiences, we replay them in our minds time and time again. Before we know it, we have had another negative encounter and begin to replay that one with all the others ones. How many times have you asked or thought "why does this keep happening to me"? It keeps happening because we keep drawing "it" to us. When we harp on negative thoughts, feelings and emotions that is what we attract to ourselves. We have to learn how to counteract every negative thought, feeling and experience with a positive thought, feeling or experience. We attract to us, what we think about the most. No matter what you feel, think positive; no matter what happens, expect positive; no matter what doors close, expect better ones to open; if your relationship fails; expect the love of your life to show up. When we think positive thoughts, make positive confessions and envision positive experiences, we send positive vibes out into the universe and that will attract and draw positive experiences to us.

Affirm & Reflect

Affirmation

*I think positively,
I speak positivity,
I am a positive being*

Reflection

Journal your thoughts on 'Positive Attraction'

Reality

While life has dealt you some blows, the reality is that if you're still alive, you have the opportunity to recover and create a better tomorrow.

Recover from what was and make the best of what is, while preparing for what will be.

To make the best of the reality that you are living now, does not mean that you don't strive for something better. It doesn't mean that you don't set goals to go further and it doesn't mean that you don't dream bigger dreams. It just simply means that you realize where you are now and that you make the best of it while in the process of moving forward. You're not pretending to have more than what you have, you're living within your means and you're planning for what's coming next. That's the way to live. Some people seem to almost get offended when you think, talk and act like your future is bigger and brighter than your present situation. Look them right in the eyes and tell them that not only do you realize exactly where you are, but more importantly, you know the reality of where you are going! They can either get on board or you can go forward without them.

Affirm & Reflect

Affirmation

*My reality
is present and future tense.
I know where I am
and I know exactly where I'm going.*

Reflection

Journal your thoughts on 'Reality'

_____

_____

_____

_____

_____

Release it and breathe...

Release it...

Release the need to be right. Release the need to be in control. Release the need to be the center. Release the need to be first. Release the need to have the last say. Release the need to be better than everyone else. Release the need to be perfect. Release the need to have a certain appearance. Release the need to be critical. Release the need to be judgmental. Release the need to force your opinion on others. Release it and just be.

Did you release it? How do you feel? I bet you can breathe again, can't you?

When you release whatever your "it" is and let it go, you make room for things to be not as you want them to be or how you forced them to appear, but as they should be.

The world of social media has become similar to reality television. Some people get all made up, make up their lives, alter the appearance of their reality but when it's time to live up to it in real life, they can't. It puts so much pressure on them and the people that they use to make their "make believe" world appear to be reality a lot of people end up angry and frustrated. What is the purpose of needing other people to think that they are something that they really aren't? That causes entirely too much stress… they need to release that and let it go.

Affirm & Reflect

Affirmation

*I release "it"
right now.
(Now close your eyes and imagine
yourself letting go)*

Reflection

Journal your thoughts on 'Release'

Remember the moments in life that captivated you and the moments that made you smile... and remember them often.

Remember the "feel good" times in life!

Too often we remember the painful moments in life. Sometimes it seems that the things that have hurt us the most or those that caused us embarrassment or shame prevail over the great moments that we've experienced.

To forget the bad times and focus on the good, may sometimes seem easier said than done. But I ask you to give it a try. Sometimes just a small shift in focus can make such a big change in perspective. Think about a good time that you had somewhere along the way in life, remember what it felt like, smile about it, reflect on it, meditate on it and while you're remembering the good things that once were, anticipate all the good that is yet to come. Don't let the bad memories, drown out the good.

Whatsoever things are true, whatsoever things are honest, whatsoever things are just, whatsoever things are pure, whatsoever things are lovely, whatsoever things are of good report; if there be any virtue, and if there be any praise, think on these things. Phil. 4:8

Affirm & Reflect

Affirmation

*I will shift my thoughts
when they become overwhelmed
with the bad and focus on the good that
is present in my life now
and that which is yet to come.*

Reflection

Journal your thoughts on 'Remember'

Rooted & Grounded

We all need a strong foundation; something to stand firm on and fall back on when need be.

Where does your foundation lie?

Life will happen to you whether you're ready for it or

not. Things change, people change, times change, people & things come and go, things happen that we have no control over…those things force us to grow, to learn, to stretch, to realize, to know what we didn't before and sometimes cause us to change direction in a moment's notice. What keeps you is what you are rooted in, where you are grounded...your foundation. With all the changes that will undoubtedly occur in our lives, we must have a strong foundation. We must have something that will keep us steady, while everything around us is uncertain. For some people it's their family unit or their belief system that keeps them strong. For me, God and the love that He has for me is my foundation. My faith is steady and strong and has been developing, building and growing since I was a child. No matter what is going on around me, I fall back on my faith. I fall back on the strength of God and that keeps me firm and steady.

Affirm & Reflect

Affirmation

*My foundation is
what keeps me grounded.
When life seems uncertain,
I will fall back on that.*

Reflection

Journal your thoughts on 'Rooted & Grounded'

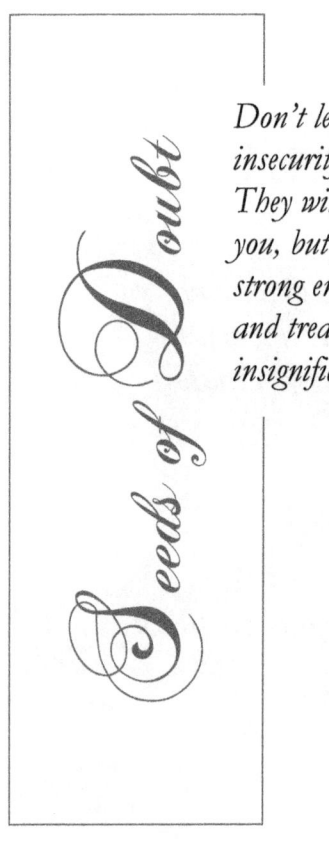

Don't let other people's insecurity become your issue. They will try to force it on you, but you have to be strong enough to recognize it and treat it just as insignificant as it is.

When people try to feed you seeds of doubt, don't chew on them and don't swallow them. Instead spit them out & keep it moving. You don't have to deal with other people's envy, jealousy, insecurity or ego issues, they do.

Affirm & Reflect

Affirmation

Repeat after me...

*Their insecurity
is not my issue nor will
I allow it to be.*

Reflection

Journal your thoughts on 'Seeds of Doubt'

Start New

It's never too late to change, it's never too late to make it right and it's never too late to begin again if that's what it takes.

You can begin again...

Things happen, relationships get rocky or they end, situations go wrong that we need to make right, we lose perspective and gain a less favorable one and the list could go on and on. Things happen that shouldn't or that we wish wouldn't have. We let too much time pass and before we know it, we don't know how we could possibly go back and make something right, that's been wrong for so long. It's never too late. It's never too late to start over, to make amends, to apologize, to work out, to work hard or change whatever needs to be changed.

If you have relationships that need mending, apologies to make or any other thing in your life to make right, go ahead and do it. As long as you are alive, you have the chance to start over again, to change directions or to reinvent yourself. It's never too late to make a new start!

Affirm & Reflect

Affirmation

*I will start today
with where I am and
with what I have.*

Reflection

Journal your thoughts on 'Start New'

Everything is subject to change. When you keep a positive Attitude.

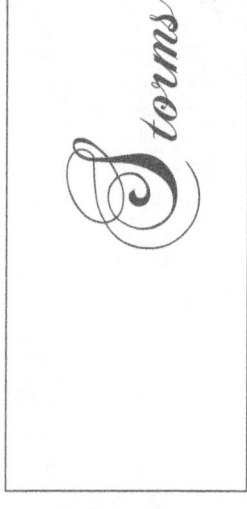

Don't stop just because you're in the middle of a storm. Keep going!

Storms will come

When you least expect it, all hell will break loose in your life and leave you standing there wondering what in the world happened, how it happened and why it happened. It doesn't matter how good, faithful, dedicated or strong you are; the storm winds will come and knock you and your efforts back 20 steps after you've just celebrated reaching step 21. When that happens, the old sayings ring true: you must weather the storm and make the choice to either sink or swim. You can't let the storms stop you, ride them out and stay focused on your destiny. The storms come to stop you, deter you, instill fear in you or cause you to doubt. It's up to you to push through the storm and keep moving toward the direction that you set out to go in. Remember that weapons will form against you, but that doesn't mean that they will prosper. That's the Word!

Affirm & Reflect

Affirmation

*Life's storms will
not stop me!*

Reflection

Journal your thoughts on 'Storms'

_____

_____

_____

_____

_____

Just as sure as storms come, they will also go

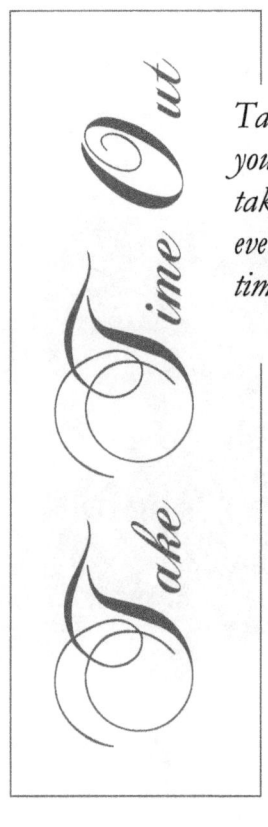

Taking time out to take care of yourself is a necessity. Don't let taking care of everyone and everything else strip you of the time needed to care for yourself.

Take some time out, to take care of you...

You do it all; take care of home, you make it happen at work, you make sure the kids are taken care of, make sure your mate is taken care of, volunteer in the community or at church, lend an ear when a friend calls, help out family when they need it, but when do you stop, step away from it all and take time out for you. Everyone needs time to recharge. If you don't take some time for yourself, you will get burned out taking care of everyone else.

Take a walk, a long drive, a visit to a local coffee shop, join a yoga or meditation class, get a hotel room for a weekend, make a visit to a vineyard, or take a trip to the beach or even out of town. Choose something that you enjoy doing and do it for you. Those that love you will understand and support you in the process. Once you get away and take some time for yourself, you'll come back refreshed and ready to jump right back in, doing all that you do for everyone else.

Affirm & Reflect

Affirmation

*I vow to myself
that I will take time out
for me.*

Reflection

Journal your thoughts on 'Take Time Out'

_____

_____

_____

_____

_____

_____

Time is precious and it's something that we can't get back. Cherish it.

Don't let wasted moments turn into years.

Wasting time, within reason, is a natural thing and we all do it from time to time. What we have to be careful of is putting off the important things and putting them off too often. Procrastination can start very small and before we know it, what we put off until tomorrow, next week or next month turns into years and years of what could have been, but never was, because we waited until it was too late. Don't waste time, value it, use it wisely and use it to your benefit to get done whatever it is that you need to do. Time can be on our side and work for us, but if we waste it, it may start working against us.

Don't be one of those people who wake up one day and see someone else fulfilling what was once your vision or living the kind of life that you could have lived if you dedicated the time and effort to make it happen. It is never too late. Start today and use every free moment that you have to make it happen!

Affirm & Reflect

Affirmation

*I value my time
too much
to waste it.*

Reflection

Journal your thoughts on 'Time'

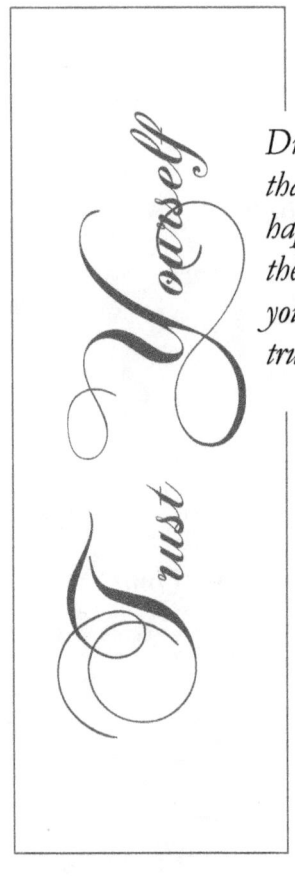

Drown out the voices telling you that you can't, that it won't happen, that it's your fault, that there is something wrong with you, that you're not enough and trust yourself.

Trust your feelings, your instincts, your thoughts, your dreams, and your intuitions.

Trust that inner voice on the inside of you. Sometimes people will try to dilute who you really are and try to feed you a convoluted version of yourself. That stems from their insecurities. You know who you are, you know what you're made of, and you know what wealth and wisdom live on the inside of you. You know yourself better than anyone else…trust in that.

Affirm & Reflect

Affirmation

*I trust my thoughts, my
intuitions, my feelings
and my actions.*

Reflection

Journal your thoughts on 'Trust Yourself'

Venture Out

Don't miss out on all that life has to offer, by staying in your comfort zone. There's more out there for you.

Sometimes it's hard to leave a place of familiarity and venture into the unknown, but how will you know what else is out there unless you take that chance.

Too often we hold on to things, places and people simply because we are familiar with them, and even though we know on the inside that it is time to let go, we either won't or just don't. Comfort, while most times a good thing, can become a hindrance when it causes us to stay right where we are because it's the easiest choice. The only way to know what else the world has to offer us is to get up, go out there and see it for ourselves. Go ahead and take that step, venture out to something new. I guarantee it will be worth it.

Affirm & Reflect

Affirmation

*I'm up for venturing
outside of my comfort zone.
I'm ready to explore all that
life has to offer me.*

Reflection

Journal your thoughts on 'Venture Out'

Dream it, see it, believe it and work hard to bring your vision to pass.

Vision is vital

Knowing where you are going in life is just as important as taking the actual steps to get there. We were not created to roam aimlessly through life without having an end-goal or destination. Life has its way of interfering with our vision, plans and goals. Sometimes life's interferences are actually nudges to get us back on track and sometimes they are hard-core knock-downs that shake us up and force us to get off the wrong track and redirect. If you don't have a vision for your life, take some time to either discover what it is or to create one. After you realize your vision, create your goals. Your goals are the steps that you take to achieve your vision. Write both your vision and your goals down and you will be on your way. Having a vision for your life is vital. Don't be tossed to and from, swaying whichever way the wind blows you. Write the vision down and make it plain, so that you can run with it. (Habakkuk 2:2 KJV)

Be more than just a person with a vision, but become one that implements it.

Affirm & Reflect

Affirmation

*I am more than a dreamer.
My dreams will become
my reality.*

Reflection

Journal your thoughts on 'Vision'

Vision... dream big and make it happen!

What

You have to give time, dedication, hard work, focus, determination, drive and commitment to really get what you want. What are you willing to give?

What are you willing to do, to get what you want, need or to where you want to be?

What are you willing to do, sacrifice, commit to, work hard at, forgive, excuse or overlook to get what you need, to reach your goals, to excel in life, to be happy, to have success, to have a successful family, to have happy functional relationships, to have financial security, to live your dreams or to see the change you want to see in your life? Sometimes we want things the easy way, we want things to just happen for us and sometimes they do. But usually we have to be willing to give more of ourselves, our time, our energy and our resources to get what we really want in life. Hard work pays off! When you do the things that you need to, for change to take place, you will start to see things in your atmosphere shift and before you know it, you will start receiving what you've been working hard to get, you will start to reap what you have sown and your efforts and sacrifice will pay off.

Affirm & Reflect

Affirmation

*I will give what it takes,
sacrifice what it takes
& do
what it takes
to achieve my goals.*

Reflection

Journal your thoughts on 'What'

Don't let anyone else define who you are. You get to determine that for yourself.

Do you know who you are? Would it surprise you that many people don't?

The truth of who a lot of people are is lost somewhere in the midst of the lies that they are living; lies that someone else told them, lies that they've told themselves and in both scenarios, the lies that they believed. It's time to peel back the layers and expose yourself for who you really are. The great, the wonderful, the awesome, the natural, the creative, the beautiful, the bruised but not broken, the hurt but yet healed, the broken hearted yet still hopeful, the believer, the dreamer, the lover, the friend, the happy, the whole, the honest, the kind, the loving, the strong, the courageous, the stronger than you knew you could be, the at peace you. It's time to reveal that person to the world. Someone out there needs THAT you. The real you…

Affirm & Reflect

Affirmation

*I will be my authentic self and not
someone else's vision of me.
I owe that to myself,
my creator and my purpose.*

Reflection

Journal your thoughts on 'Who are You'

Who Said

Don't focus on what "they" say about you. Your opinion outweighs "theirs" every time.

I'm sorry, who said what...?

Who said you couldn't do it, who said you didn't measure up, who said you weren't good enough, who said you weren't attractive enough, who said you weren't smart, who said you weren't capable, who said you couldn't handle it, who said you were too tall or too short or too skinny or too fat…who said? Who said it and why did they say it? Sometimes people say things to you based on their own insecurities, but you have to remember that just because they said it doesn't make it true and it doesn't make it your reality.

My question to you is what do YOU say? What did God say? It seems to me that those are the only two opinions that really matter.

Affirm & Reflect

Affirmation

*I am who God says I am,
I am who I say I am
and that is more
than enough.*

Reflection

Journal your thoughts on 'Who Said'

Words are a powerful force. Choose to speak words that create positive outcomes instead of negative ones.

Words can hurt but they can also heal.

Words are a powerful force that can change the atmosphere, change your heart and shift your world. Use your words to create and not destroy, to bless and not curse, to help and not hinder, to love and not hate, to uplift and not tear down, to build and not break, to create peace and not chaos. God said and He saw and if we are created in His image and likeness we have the ability to do the same. Whether we see the results of what we speak immediately or not doesn't mean that we aren't creating something with the words that we speak. Make it a point to use the power of your words to create and to reach, teach and touch lives.

Affirm & Reflect

Affirmation

*I use the power of
my words to create, to reach,
to teach and to touch lives.*

Reflection

Journal your thoughts on 'Words'

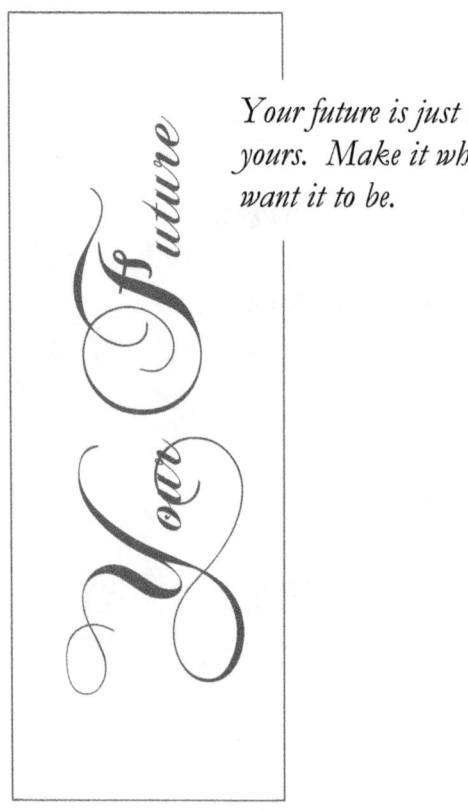

Your future is just that, yours. Make it what you want it to be.

Your future is not lost because of your past.

Don't compare your future with your past, your past is already written BUT your future is a blank page...an open canvas...so write/paint/create something beautiful.

Affirm & Reflect

Affirmation

*The best is yet to come
and I have the ability to create
something amazing for
my life.*

Reflection

Journal your thoughts on 'Your Future'

There may be times when you question it, but just know that the Creator is always near. Omnipotent & Omnipresent.

God is There

When you're disappointed in yourself
God is still there, cheering you on
When you lose someone you love
God is still there
When your friends/family turn on you
God is still there
When you get sick
God is still there
When you lose your job
God is still there
During your struggle
God is still there
When you're in pain
God is still there
When you're confused
God is still there
When you've been wronged
God is still there
When you can't see your way clear
God is still there
When your dream dies
God is still there, with a new one
When your heart breaks
God is still there
When your finances are in trouble
God is still there
When life gets hard
God is still there
When you doubt Him
God is still there

When it doesn't feel like He's there
God is still there.

Though the NOISE in your head is loud, it is not louder than God, He is still there. Remember when He healed your body, promoted you, saved you, answered your prayers, gave you a million second chances after you couldn't get the first 999,999 quite right, loved you when you didn't love yourself, sent people to minister to you and pray for you in your darkest hour, healed your relationships, removed those people from your life that shouldn't have been there in the first place, opened doors for you when it seemed like they were all bolted shut, sent people to help you when you didn't know where to turn, blessed you with wonderful friends, introduced you to the perfect person FOR YOU, gifted you with only a gift that He can give, gave you those beautiful children, nephews & nieces, protected you in times that you didn't even know you were being protected, kept you in your right mind when you wanted to lose it, surrounded you with His presence when you needed a hug, made "it" possible when everything seemed impossible, made the sun shine on a rainy day just to let you know that He was there…so remember when it doesn't feel like He is anywhere around…God IS There.

God is there

Don't lose faith.
God has not forgotten you.
When it's all said and done, just make sure that you
don't forget yourself.

Breathe in new, invigorating, inspiring, hope-filled,
determined Breaths of Life…and Begin Again.

Erika Morgan
EMagine That Creations LLC
emaginethat@live.com

Erika Morgan is a freelance writer from Detroit, Michigan. She draws from life's experiences, those that have been and those that she believes can be; to inspire, motivate and encourage her readers.

Note from the Author:

Some dreams take a long time to be fulfilled, but that doesn't mean that they won't happen. Against hope, keep believing in hope, keep believing in yourself, keep believing in your dreams, keep believing that you will and keep knowing that you can. There will be times when you feel like you are walking alone, but keep walking. Eventually you'll meet the right people along the way. It may feel like no one is there to encourage you, and if you find that to be the case, encourage yourself and meet yourself at the finish line. Love.

Erika

www.ingramcontent.com/pod-product-compliance
Lightning Source LLC
Chambersburg PA
CBHW051649040426
42446CB00009B/1051